Contents

Foreword
Streams of Consciousness
Supermoon
Occupation
Michael Brendan Hanmore
Life Intimidating Art
Giraffe
Falcon Queue
Mrs Maguire
Environoego.com
Quintessence
Dating Site Hell
Beatles Fan Insect Scandal
Totem and Taboo
Anybody seen Ashy
Ode to Joy
Death Warmed Up
Canterbury Trails
The Ontological Argument

To King Carlos

' Carl Stipetic awesome repertoire
cubase in yer face Ziggy played guitar '

Cheers dude

Tony

Foreword

Once upon a time there was a man with no arms
Who was being chased by a swarm of bees
So he jumped into a pond
And hid under the water
Until the angry bees had buzzed past overhead

When he got out he was hungry
So he ate two hot dogs a loaf of bread and two bananas
Then turned around and laughed aloud
At the profound hound in the panorama

• Cho (noun) – God-like self

Streams of Consciousness

I am Barry Normal also known as average Joe
Non-descript ordinary from head to toe
That felt compelled to take up ones pen
Let creative juices flow

For your perusal a collection of odes
And carefully crafted anecdotes
Verbal outpourings throw away quotes
Rhymes and misdemeanours smatterings of dodgy prose

The musings of an ape man home alone in Scholes
A cracked actor that fluffed his best lines
Scuppered the roles
Exotic herbs a play on words
Poetry in motion dragged over hot coals
There is nothing either good or bad
But thinking makes it so

I am self-aware the only one I know
37 trillion cells of throbbing gristle cho
Welcome to my one man band imagination show
Intense self-reflection a precise introspection live from the
Pleasure dome

Sex sensuality Riemann's Hypothesis
I employed the literary technique of parataxis
Took the sum of all the parts turned them into this
An explanation exploration of an epic mid-life crisis so it is

Zarathustra my heart Almustafa my soul
Prometheus gave fire led me in from the cold
From out of the depths of a terrible despair
Phoenix like I rose
To speak of truth the hardest lesson learned
Hell it have no rage like love to hatred turned

Ecstatic flights burial sites warts and all no compromise
Xenophanes trilobites to engage energise
I made it all up as I went along sometime did plagiarise
In advance I apologise to those of youse that own the
Copyrights

In my defence I say that qubit deconstruction reconstructed
That offers an insight
Into the rapid expansion of an externalised mind
From the point of view of the light
Its self doth justify

So without further ado let me introduce to you
Spectacular vernacular awkward portmanteaus
There's a fly in the ointment stuck in the groove
A bee in my bonnet twice I removed
The service here is terrible likewise the food
Waiter! there are streams of consciousness
In this doggerel soup

Supermoon

One day the earth sat in blissful repose
Gazing at the sun

If only the sun and I could be closer
Then more perfect would be the eternal day
She said to the moon

The moon stopped from pulling the tides
Thought for a moment then spoke

Not too hot not too cold
Not too young nor too old
Not too near like Venus
Not too far like Mars

Not in the immediate vicinity of supernovas
Or in close proximity to binary stars
No need for change when things are just right
Precisely as they are

The earth felt gladdened was no longer saddened
And the moon returned to making waves
As though nothing had happened

Good morning starshine
The earth she says hello

Occupation

I attended my youngest daughter's open evening at primary
School to check up on her progress
Discuss any other issues with minimum fuss
Her teacher appeared shook my hand smiled said hello I'm
Mrs Guest
Then proceeded to speak of realpolitik high percentage
Groups a recital of government statistics
And league tables quickly ensued
Your little girl is bright polite good attendance pleasant
Attitude I stifled my own contribution not wishing to be rude

Suddenly she closed the book shut glanced a cursory look
As if she were weighing me up
Broke with convention her big friendly eyes held my attention
Then with kindly intention asked a rhetorical question
Mr Fallon what do you do for a living?

I am an electrician I replied slightly taken aback
One bad moment away from a panic attack
I'm on the defensive as a matter of fact

Well that's not what your daughter thinks please follow me
Presented for my inspection a wall of drawings
A children's art gallery
Pointed at one in particular said this is what she believes
Turned quickly on her heels vanished into mist

I gazed upon a picture of a spindly smiley man
White teeth red lips pink cheeks
With eyes and ears bendy arms wavy hands
Stood beside a light commercial van

Black trousers raven hair big fun sized boots
He looked kind of ugly but in a way kind of cute

Wearing a blue tee shirt with a dazzlingly bright fusion of
Light exploding from his heart
And behind him in the background lay a vast array of
Twinkling little stars

High up in the heavens a mellow yellow sun did float
Underneath this pleasant scene a child's hand had wrote
My Dad lights up the world

Ha ha that's me that's who she imagines me to be
Wow what a responsibility
For a good while I stood and stared
At no such thing as impossibility
Others tell us who we are
As far as one can see

It's fair to say that I felt a whole lot better leaving there
Than way back in the day
A white van man is who I am
Next stop the milky way

Michael Brendan Hanmore

South of the river St Joseph's Club
Hid between houses maisonettes towers of dub
Hemmed in by flyovers arterial roads industrial hub
Licensed to sell intoxicants to Tommy Wass and Peggy Tub
The scene is set for a gathering of the Hunslet old Boys
Lapsed Catholic bruddahood related by blood
To reflect pay respect acknowledge the death of a matriarch
Pure in heart lest we forget

She was light gave life to formless shapes
Universal love did advocate
Showered affection upon gormless reprobates
Courage quiet dignity cruel twists of fate
Tried condemned merciful end
Shook a seven ascended into heaven
It wasn't the cough that carried her off
It was the coffin they carried her off in

His sister my mother
I pulled up a chair and sat before the other
Face to face with Dionysus no handshake nor greeting kiss
Fragile peace perchance to speak rewrite history say our piece
Zeitgeist spirit of the times midsummer 2007
This is how it feels to be lonely

Hedonist 40 years on the piss
A heaving scuzzy mass of seething masculinity
Drowning in potions of cider and ice
Shaking like a shiting dog before my very eyes
Demon drink Lily the Pink working class nemesis
Addiction physical dereliction
A shadow of the man John Patrick and I once idolised

A drunkard man is a mad man
The lunatic has taken over the asylum
Hooded youth to the left of me ugly brutes to the right
Here I am stuck in the middle with you
Relax stay cool when in Rome do as they do
Patches I'm depending on you son to pull the family through

Puzzle enigma mystery
He was my role model eleven harsh winters the elder of me
Could mimic WC Fields convincingly
Persistence of memory Les Dawson Dick Emery
Reflections on the way life used to be

When I was a boy this man was king
Followed his example verbatim
Male chauvinist pig perverted by language
Hey fatty bum bum sweet sugar dumpling
Faith of our fathers living still
Speak when spoken to answer when called
On a need to know basis they wont tell us sod all
Morphic resonance genetic inheritance throw one in the mix
I got my own guilt trip to live with and he got his
To be a good man is a discipline

Mythical status worshipped adored
He has forgotten more then we know
Never walk on quicksand don't eat yellow snow
Introduced scrabble and chess the Mandelbrot set
World of Sport shock and awe
To mindless automatons straight out of Whinmoor
Got well peeved when our kid spelled down the word quaver
On a triple word score
Back then he was Mikie life and soul of the party
Before Micko his pikey alter ego got a grip took a hold

Waited on spoiled rotten an ungrateful son of a gun
A total waste of space if ever there was one
Mother Mary's proverbial pain in the bum
Threw away the best bits kept the ectoplasm
An angry young adult an accident waiting to happen
Known to promote negative agendas
Prone to bellicose outbursts of withering sarcasm
After all day benders

World in Action Play for Today
Never met a cockney that didn't know the Krays
Watching TV fiddling with dials
Trying to find the Rockford Files
All the whilst eating scran from a plate on a tray
Man Alive I will Survive please thyself the order of the day
The earth's a big blue marble when you see it from out there

Brandy and port too easily bored
The best footballer I never saw play
Hung up his boots aged n n n n nineteen
To concentrate on ale
Fatally flawed My Sweet Lord
Couldn't be arsed to pick up a guitar
Strike a chord from Ibiza to the Norfolk Broads

Bad mazzle on the razzle up the shirkers down with recession
Dashing out for a full on boozy schmoozy session
In the tap room of the Grey Goose public house free
Admission
To meet Arch and Stan Charlie Chan Flash in the Pan
Checking out Jethro Tull Yusaf Islam
Beer and fags Oxford Bags high heel shoes low neck sweater
Life is a shit sandwich the more bread the better

Time flies memories light the corners of my mind
Some bizzare I went to the bar pulled myself to one side
How did high and mighty meet such demise

The barmaid momentarily derailed my train of thought
Asked me what I'd like
Can I get a witness a voice for those that have no voice
I wearily enquired
There are no answers only choices verily she replied
But just to make it interesting we'll have a shilling on the side

Jump to the beat the lion speaks I returned to my seat
Double diamond works wonders for umpalumpas
In aran wool jumpers
That clumsily spill frothing pints of pain relief
Over leopard skin sneakers
Drenching the charcoal odor eaters of dodgy looking geezers
I really love your Tiger Feet

Our conversation was short and bleak
Endless cycles of despair destined to repeat
Beyond repair a culture immersed in alcohol
Vitriol cannibal ritual
If it's good enough for Jesus Christ
Then it's good enough for me
Feels like I'm just a dream in the mind of some deity
It's in my nature to be cynical

Accident of birth Who Wants The World?
He could've been the rogue classicist
That unravelled the Voynich manuscript
If circumstances were different
I don't consider myself superior to him in any sense
Diss the bigots not the victims
Live in the past die in the past
Nothing endures like the human condition

Too late baby now its too late
Open up the floodgates perish under waves
A new storm is looming uncle dysfunctional
Drinks himself an early grave
A wise man has the power to reason away

It's a Greek tragedy a family affair
We prodigal sons with nothing left to say
Go on then cho fuck off he cried in despair
And I would rather be anywhere else than here today

I said goodbye to Katie Jo hoped that she take care
As I turned to leave felt deflated disconfigurated
For the future scared

Choked provoked crisis mode
Never meet your idol nothing queerer than folk
Found my way outside had a smoke
Somebody spoke and I went into a dream
Once again the power of the herb open up the mind
A single leaf not yellow without the knowledge of the tree
Nostalgia aint what it used to be
I'm finished with the past but it aint done with me

All is not good in da hood
The mighty have fallen the city is gone
Two vast trunkless legs stand on the site
Of this forgotten Babylon where Colossus once stood
End of days these remain
Faith hope tough love

Fenian scum our day has come
Barbarians run amok in our dominion
The famine is over nothing left of the farm
Mere words are unnecessary they can only do harm

Life Intimidating Art

Cave drawings severed heaven
God is dead 9/11
Ventriloquists with depression
Don't want to set a bad impression

Outline sketch steps retraced
A sucker for a pretty face
Da da da cut and paste
Artistic licence waste of space

Breaking Bad the Iliad
The motherland colossus of Volgograd
These dreams in which I'm dying
Are the best I've ever had

Never complain revulse convulse
Set the bulls of Pamplona loose
Never explain distort confuse
Act on impulse join in the abuse

Philip Roth jerking off
Semen stains seared into cloth
Nervous energy smokers cough
Midnight oil writers block

Patronage royal decree
Paranoia third degree
The defendant in the trial of the century
Stands accused of heresy
For outraging public decency
And having the audacity to think freely

A man of Dutch origin ripped off his own ear
The more that you suffer the more you endear
Under the cosh an appointment with fear
The charge of the light brigade Ligetis atmospheres
Grotesque caricatures Kilroy was here

Fuck art let's dance
A standing prick knows no conscience
Methinks ethics are a nonsense
Peace breaks out violence transcends
Artisans new romantic partisans
Join hands around The Wicker Man

The indigenous people of South America
Could not see the Conquistador ships
Because a word to describe them did not exist
Rendering them powerless to resist
The onslaught of death cult activists
Every picture tells a story that goes beyond the infinite
Art for art's sake say culture vultures through hysterical lips

Suspended animation locked in a vault a threat to creation
The last small pox virus sleeps in deep hibernation
Dreams of release golden fleece feeling at ease
To wipe out civilisation continue the endless relentless battle
Between life and annihilation

Art imitates life
Life intimidates art
Illumination free expression
Enough to break a lover's heart

Giraffe

I am having a bath with a giraffe shaking off the riggers
Reflecting on the vigours of a hard days graft
A candle is lit the door it is shut
To keep out the draft and Jabba the Hutt

I'm sharing a bath with a Masai giraffe
Switched off the data streams laid back chillaxed
A glass of wine maybe a carafe
Enjoying the fruits of our labour
Savouring the flavour of the grapes of wrath

I was causing a splash with a tipsy giraffe
Both coming to terms with the fact
That here and now is where we are at
When suddenly from out of nowhere a hippopotamus
Appeared with a crate full of beer
Whose friendly smile cheery disposition
All at once they endeared
It's frothy man

Upon his head sat a tiny pair of twitching ears
That old father time humorously designed
And mother nature tongue in cheek tweaked refined
Ever so slowly over eons of sublime

Hey I've got an idea he excitedly said
Let's build a raft an amphibious craft
Sail away to the land of the daft
Where odds and goods are always stacked
Mindless violins gratuitous sax
Large elephants jump slowly sink rapidly
Never mind the bollocks spend and tax

The camelopardalis the fellow with the long neck was
Perturbed by the dumbest thing he ever heard
A ridiculous notion truly absurd
Clearly disturbed something inside of him stirred
Then looking down from high above uttered these words
Some they hunt in packs others run with herds
Some are carnivores the rest are herbivores
In the great circle of life 3.142 always recurs
A thing only exists when its body swerves
Why kill two birds with one stone
When one can get stoned with two
Let's stay put in Lilliput my advice to you

The river horse without any force felt inclined to agree
With the focal points from the discourse
At which time I submerged submarine like slipped beneath
The warm soapy water to reconsider Murphy's Law

Ted Hughes Sylvia Plath a gravestone epitaph
Two barmy bar stewards drove each other mad
Even amidst fierce flames the golden lotus can be planted
Inscribed by blade light luminous black
Flexing like the lens of a mad eye
Gone are the dark clouds that had me blind

I'm still in Iraq with Fleetwood and Mac
Testing our fault conditions to see how we react
We are shapeshifters we can adapt
To preserve our modesty the inglorious three
Wear trunks in the bath

Oh how we all laughed danced goofed around
To the wah guitar sound of Isaac Hayes' theme from Shaft
Insanity is to attempt to swim against the tide
Whilst soaking in a bubble bath
Augustine of Hippo that joke isn't funny anymore
Yer 'aving a giraffe.

Falcon Queue

Falcon Electrical Wholesalers Sheepscar Street Leeds
Sell goods to Joe Public and the wider industry
Every kind of spoken language every kind of ethnicity
Step inside wait a while and you'll be served eventually

Stock all types give the best price is their philosophy
The customer is always wrong the queue is legendary
The drinks machine has run out of chocolate
Undrinkable the tea
The coffee tastes disgusting but hey at least it's free

John is the owner a man true to his word
The sound of his raucous laughter
Is joyously absurd often heard
He and Raj his brother named the business
After a hunting bird
Then a parting of ways somehow occurred

When top dog is away Martin calls the shots
He's been here forever long ago lost the plot
He had hair down to his arse
Way back in the days that time forgot
Drove a battered brown metro all over town
Waiting For Godot

Pile it high sell it cheap everything must go
Dennis and Paul remind me of the critics
On the Muppet Show
Please say it aint so my resistance is low
As the opening refrain from tears of a clown
Plays out on the radio

Vexed Caucasians perplexed Asian dudes
3 times divorced electricians in contemplative moods
Bored apprentices stare at phones wear trendy running shoes
Together stand in line with 4 foot 6 inch druids
Clutching 5 foot tubes

Presidential candidate's influential heads of state
The pace is always slow the flow is more sedate
For chavs and spivs alike even the Emir of Kuwait
The golden rule in here is everyone must wait

Sarcastic Ricky takes no prisoners cuts no ice
Freely gives helpful tips on wireless kits
Sound advice on augur bits to the assembled boring tools
Stares into your eyes looking for lies
Grudgingly issues refunds for damaged goods when
Completely satisfied

Whatever happened to Gil nobody will tell
No one knows where Noah is cos he's a law unto himself
So we the captured audience in desperation must sometimes
Serve ourselves
Meanwhile back of stage Sean is ordering 12v batteries
For a Buddhist terror cell

Someone down the line is moaning on about the NICEIC
Earth electrodes KA ratings requirements for PME
'Ere mate if it's in the 18th Edition
Then who are we to disagree
What the flux the value of Ze got to do with me?

Ginger John with shiny head a whiter shade
That's sometimes red
Still haunted by the shenanigans of Peter, Cooper, Fred
He changes the till roll twice a day then goes back to bed
No one bothers to tell him that really he is dead

Nick the fork lift driver covered in tattoos
John and Neil the new starters bewildered confused
When Mangal in a tangle finally returns from his heroic quest
With the wrong kind of fuse
Whilst the rest of us gathered here look on thoroughly
Unamused

Simon and David they work in accounts
Calculating discounts adding VAT to net amounts
Laid back pleasant attitudes which is kind of surprising
Considering the sheer volume of invoice disputes
Terms and conditions abuse they manage to sort out

Polish Max couldn't cope with stir crazy
Retrained became a plumber went in search of Royston Vasey
Someone said he was lazy but the details were hazy
The terminator moved on to greener pastures
Hasta la vistalux baby

Pandora's Box was opened bedlam was unleashed
The cleaner mops and slops around the feet
Of the easily displeased
The devil keeps away God can't stand the heat
I like to think that Danny and Daz the drivers
Are in a better place now may they rest in peace

Tony Bright Sparks I am known as in here
I have been stood around waiting for many a year
Now at long last the gear I ordered has finally appeared
I went in closely shaven and came out with a beard
So as one shepherd said to the other
Let's get the flock out of here

Mrs Maguire

40 years loyal service mother of the school
Months away from retirement well deserved overdue
Made time for those with needs the most
Not just a chosen few
Listened without prejudice gave good advice to busy fools
She was heard to speak highly of the girl
With the dragon tattoo

Blue eyes blond hair Abbaesque glamour
Taught Spanish grammar with a slight stammer genuinely
Loved by pupils old and new
I know a lot about her because she taught my sister
Both my daughters and way back in days of old
When knights were bold she was my teacher too

Yes she had detractors was known to nag and moan
One person's motivator another person's crone
But what possessed a year 11 boy to commit the gravest sin
She never could have known
Hence the seeds were scattered murderous barbs have grown
A hard rain's gonna fall where brutality shards were sown

He struck without warning stuck to the task
Hid his intention behind an implacable mask
No one could prevent the outbreak of madness
And those that may have harboured doubts or vague
Inclinations as to the seriousness of the situation
Put it down to teenage angst youthful bombast
For all the wrong reasons we are now on the map

Repeatedly stabbed in the neck the back
Knifed to death in front of her class
Terrified children witness the attack
Don't let them see me die she gasped
Then into the arms of a colleague collapsed
Where was her saviour in her hour of need
An anguished people ask

Word of the atrocity quickly spilled out
Sending seismic shock waves throughout the town
Stunned horrified the local community organised
And rallied round
Multitudes came to pay tribute share common ground
To show the watching wider world that love it still abounds

A sea of flowers to fences tied
The bloom of youth hugged and cried
Feeling the hurt footballers wore Maguire 61
On the backs of their shirts
United in grief too numb to speak
The desensitised crowd set balloon lanterns free to drift
Into boundless azure skies
Spirited away

Sky news court update a juvenile takes centre stage
This was no tragic accident no defence to make
Plain simple the motive was hate
No apologies were offered no excuses made
When pressed for a reason life is good he proclaimed

Left it to his father my lifelong friend a good and decent man
To try explain away
Left it to his family to unfairly bear the burden of shame
The focal point of public outrage a slap in the face
For all the countless acts of selfless devotion
Made in his name
That sinking feeling could things have been done differently
Were they somehow to blame

Left to the victim's husband and loved ones
A cross of catastrophic loss to carry forever and a day
Twilight years together cruelly snatched away
How could such terrible tragedy happen in God's school
Et tu Brute?
Beauty is fleeting actions remain

Horses for courses maddening bureaucratic forces
Why the need for veils of secrecy and gagging clauses
Full disclosure it is vital to know if more should have been
Done to protect her from a pupil who was known
To be plotting her murder

What of the background noise from previous confrontations
The deadly chain of events that led to her demise
What lessons to be learnt from this ghastly enterprise
That even in death her rights are recognised
So we the traumatised can find some kind of closure
Help restore peace of mind somehow draw a line
Underneath the gory story the day the music died

April 28th 2014 end of an era end of a dream
A new date in the calendar of infamy
Brutal fact devils pact twas indeed a heinous act
But if evil is tangible the abominable real
Is it wrong to believe that somewhere inside the firestorm of
This epic theodicy an opposite of yin must also be

What are we to do with what are we to make
Of the boy that took a life threw his own away
A figure of hate no release date
A notorious killer held indefinitely in captured state
Will we ever hear an act of contrition remorseful confession
We'll just have to wait

Years ago it was common for schools to be named
After inspirational people deemed good and kind
Illustrious luminaires shoulders to the grind
Gave all to the cause died for the faith
Alas nowadays beatitudes have changed
Joan of Arc St Thomas Becket would turn in the grave
To see such fall from grace

What shall her legacy be how best to remember her by
To honour such exemplary service supreme sacrifice
Aspire set the bar higher what is life but to walk between
Great fires·rename the school Anne Maguire
Louder louder as if we had a choice
In the meantime a small plaque on an obscure departmental
Wall must suffice
Out of sight out of mind

A few weeks before she was murdered
I was called out in a professional capacity
To my alma mater Corpus Christi High School Neville Road
East Leeds
When she stopped me on the stairs to speak
Tell your beautiful girls that I love them
Her last words spoken to me

Beguiled tongue-tied I meekly smiled made no reply
Stood and watched her walk on by
Then I turned down the corridor to meet
Kevin Lambert and Bernard Butterfield the caretakers
To figure out a way to fix the failing of the lights
Swapped a joke shared a laugh
Oblivious to the fact that we were about to be
Plunged into darkness
Engulfed by such horror the combined minds of
Edgar Allan Poe and Mary Shelley
Could not have summoned up

Exegesis
The truth is thus
A parable for modern times
Chaos reigns in paradise
So say all of us

Environoego.com

Is

A diverse scientific social political video sharing
Community that addresses local and global
Environmental issues

We advocate the sustainable management of resources and
Stewardship of the environment through peaceful changes in
Public policy and individual behaviour

Environoego recognises that humanity is a participant not an
Enemy of ecosystems. Our ideas are centred on ecology
Health education human and animal rights
And the protection of endangered species.

We are friends of the environment citizens of the earth
Who question the perceived wisdom of unsustainable
Economic growth
We believe in a free market
Respect the rights of the individual to create wealth
But not in an all-consuming monster neither principled
Nor ethical that serves only itself

We are not fanatics or extremists
We are free thinkers fair minded agents of change
That seek to raise environmental awareness
Open new dialogues engage in discussions stimulate debate

We aim to influence popular opinion
With well-reasoned discourse
We stand for common sense and non-violent protest
Our ultimate goal is to protect the planet
From the worst of mankind's excess

Together we are not powerless
We are an irresistible force

Quintessence

Music
The vital impulse
The fifth classic element
The most perfect embodiment of consciousness and nature

I am a poet I am a musician
A part time magician full time adherent of the Tesla tradition
That evoked the noego Quintessence
Out of the ether into existence
A quintessential sing along 50 song repertoire
Viva la resistance

No audience glare zero fanfare
An in depth analysis on the whys and wherefores
Of tortoises and hares
Detailing the sonic adventures of a space cadet
On a perilous mission
That deals with the aftermath toxic fall out
From a great war of attrition
In a 5 album set from just a position

Songs of desolation with nihilistic themes
The flaw of attraction broken down dreams
Cringing scenes selfish genes every rhythm of that virtuosity
Jukebox jive marital strife all points in between

Popular culture organised sound
Messed around with tempo beats and catchy maladies
In search of the profound
Went out to work each day to pay the bills
Both feet on the ground

Written from the ringside with laughs along the way
The underdog against the odds somehow made the grade
An act of God a Manichean play
A fluke a happy accident some may say
Zippa de do da serendipity day

For general amusement it includes Disney spells looney tunes
Extreme mood swings romantic interludes
And for lovesick individuals a different kind of blues

Tall stories morbid fascinations
Bad vibes good vibrations
The travelogue of a small cog
In an immense musical machination

An antidote some aural relief
A comfort blanket in an empty state of disbelief
To ward off the worst effects of
Chronic loneliness and compassion fatigue
An exit strategy for when your boat has sprung a leak
And you find yourself without a paddle
Whilst canoeing up shit creek
Orbiting the sun not having much fun
At 66,000 miles per hour as we speak

On the go music chorus and verse
The sublime the ridiculous the downright absurd
Mind over matter the use of will power
To overcome personal problems and spiritual dilemmas

Carl Stipetic awesome repertoire
Cubase in yer face Ziggy played guitar
Out of dark matter an existential noir
From edge of empire a muso's account of the story thus far
Boney was a warrior Jean Francois

Nowhere to run nowhere to hide
Who are you not to shine in the light?
Rough justice soundtracks for life
A users guide on how to survive the rollercoaster ride
When the eternal universe attempts quantum suicide
Stand well back hold on tight
Just because you're breathing it don't mean that you're alive

Dating Site Hell

Text carefully all ye that enter in

Wild thing Suzy Guru
Paula Hot Love big fan of La Roux
One click away waiting for you
Subscribe exercise your consumer rights to pick and choose
Everyone's a winner babe that's the truth

A man's got to do what a man's got to do
I aint getting no love got nothing to lose
And right now I'm hornier than a bull rampaging through
The brass section of Barry White's Love Unlimited orchestra
Whilst in session
No point in being a poet if words can't seduce
The following events occurred around the time Ashley
Madison made the news

Hello how are you today how did you end up in here?
In blind panic I scrambled up some lame excuse hoped it
Came across sincere
Morning glory a cover story I'm a little green behind the ears
Oblivious to the nuances unwritten rules
Of the dating site Blues

A friend with benefits open minded open ended
Works with the elderly cares for the demented
She took offence at some perceived indifference where none
Was intended hit the panic button I was unfriended

Stop and chat don't be shy let's talk awhile
Wrote Sexy Princess Ruth
So without hesitation I struck up a conversation
About my fascinations flirting with emoticons
I sensed she understood

Then with no word of warning
From point of contact was removed

Ghosted rebuked machismo deflated
No fool like an old fool with something still to prove
In an act of desperation born of frustration
To brighten up my Situation
I sought solace with Tracey one nine seven two
Alas my friendship request was ignored denied
Nevermind c'est la vie the seagulls follow the trawler
Because there are plenty more fish in the sea
I am starting to think that everyone else in cyber space
Is having a better time than me

What about blonde bombshell the one with trust issues
That voluptuous lady in the low cut top
A fabulous vision of complete womanhood
With anti EU views
Feeling neglected misunderstood
Likes country music kangaroos caribous
Is looking for her soul mate to live happily ever after with
In a land called Xanadu

Doesn't want a casual relationship needs full commitment
Maybe more
At night time she likes to feel fine
Imbibe on the fruit of the vine
Watch Netflix pics liggin' out on scatter cushions strewn
Across the floor
Got rid of the husband couldn't stand him anymore
Genuine guys only please she's been hurt before

Bonjour nomenclature my name is Earl
I got everything but the girl
You can stay at my fixed abode or I could come to yours
And boomphh just like that two worlds collided

Through social intercourse
We met up on the Saturday no funny stuff of course
Declared our love on Sunday Monday we divorced

Juicy Lucy Rita Patel there to catch me if I fell
Yorkshire Rose Bridlington Belle lonely Jo with lots to tell
We interact with each other in dating site hell
Dancing to algorhythms within the echo chambers of the
Internet of things
Typo errors Freudian slips the absence of full stops and
Apostrophes
Catfish flat screen virtual relationships
Can't ascertain for certain if these people exist

No mannerisms or personality clues
No idiosyncratic twitches from which to deduce
Consenting adults have broken with tradition
Severed ties with social conservatism
Mary Whitehouse attitudes
If two people stalk each other which one is zooming who?
Hell is other people one can reasonably assume

There are so many lonely hearts in here
The administrators can't lose
We can cancel our direct debits any time they choose
The oldest swingers in town set free again
To put their heads back in the noose
Play with wi-fire in the shires
Because there's nothing better else to do

Bad habits rampant rabbit's schadenfreude bad karma
Peaches and cream tangerine dream hyenas piranhas
Misogynists and misandrists wrapped up in body armour
Cheap thrills enhancement pills
Set the backdrop to big pharma

You have a delicious sense of irony seem so laid back
I like those qualities in a man wrote Curvy Cherie
The reason for that I replied is mostly I'm out of my tree
Trying not to take the absurdity of life too seriously
A borderline recluse footloose fancy free
I go where the music takes me but draw the line at Radio 3

Paint a picture describe yourself tell me what you want and
Who you are
She don't mind risqué or double entendre
Man of leisure under pressure made to measure ribbed for
Pleasure I messaged back to her

To my relief she text back right away to say
That was the funniest thing she'd read all week
Went on to add
How much she admired my bare faced cheek
A person with a perverse sense of humour
Wildly overactive imagination is exactly what she seeks
Yes indeed to another level let us proceed

OMG a result I've only gone and pulled
Somehow my comedy of errors has entertained
Kept her amused
We share epic conversations fully clothed sometimes nude
When I squint at her blurred profile photo
She resembles Penelope Cruise
We are meeting up in 3D real soon me myself will introduce
If all goes well can bid farewell
To dating site hell and social media blues

Beatles Fan Insect Scandal

There is nothing more annoying than a disorientated fly
Constantly crashing into doors bouncing off of walls
Colliding with venetian blinds
All the while emitting an angry band saw ear piercing grind
That grates and irritates and drives one out of one's mind

A bitter end a sad demise
Any last prayers before you die
I am a Titan with the power to decide
And you are small fry
A carrier of parasitic protozoa and e-coli
I give you fair warning that the swat team has been mobilised

But what good be gained satisfaction derived
If I was to exterminate the only other witness
To this comedy divine
I am your observer and you in turn are mine
Planes of existence we can each verify

So I have unrolled the snoozepaper
Set aside the initial desire to spray insecticide
A noble beast an instrument of thy peace
Could not hurt a fly
St Francis of Assisi would understand the reason why

Homosapien magic fly
A thousand twinkles in each compound bug eye
In eureka moment metamorphosized left unhappiness behind
Beatles fan insect scandal
Was splashed across the front page of the Fortean Times

Totem and Taboo

Teenage rampage lager lout rage
Two sheets to the wind penned in behind barricades
A chavalanche surging down the stand
Shouting menacing threats hurling obscenities
Across the no-man's land

Skinheads flickheads assorted dickheads
Gesticulate at rival fans
Sing bawdy songs make shameful racist and disgraceful
Sexist chants then swear allegiance to eleven desperate Dans
Hard-core uproar we are here to spoil the party
Upset the master plan

We don't use polite insults like butterfingers or buffoon
Our words are weapons we too frequently misuse
Most of us from poor backgrounds a few with silver spoons
Together we take diabolical liberties
To keep ourselves amused

Hark now hear United sing the scum they ran away
We don't let minor things like historical accuracy
Spoil the drama of the play
The only film we've seen this year is Kes
A Kestrel for a Knave
And there will be a massacre upon this Saturday

We are extremely loathsome when we gather in large groups
The referee's a wanker the opposition must be abused
We roam around have no fear
Shag our women drink our beer
Might get done but never run
You daren't come over here

Opposing fans speak in grunts
A proper weird looking bunch of scruffy runts
At half time they propose to their ugly birds
Over indulge in stupid cupid stunts
Egged on by their local radio disc jockey
Who didn't make the cut on Pebble Mill at One

Under the Influence of Spartacus and Quadrophenia
Plus copious amounts of Hanna Barbera psychedelia
Enjoying the buzz of psychofan hysteria
We quite fancy Florence not so Fiorentina
You'll never walk alone with schizophrenia

Oh no say it aint so the baying mob as one we groan
Some worzel has grabbed the winner with minutes left to go
A 30 yard screamer that nearly broke the net
The spawny little scrote
That bearded freak who likes northern soul
Featured in last month's edition of Shoot and Goal
He likes steak and chips Bernard Manning and the
Love Thy Neighbour show

A bloodthirsty crew with restricted view
Disarray affray about to break loose
And judging by the levels of over enthusiasm
Shown by the local plod it seems safe to conclude
That the police like a bit of a do too
Get paid generous overtime rates enough to fill their boots
They treat us like animals then wonder why it is
We try take over the zoo

Bobbys helmets sarcastic grins tight leather straps
Narrow eyes double chins
Wielding truncheons steaming in
Lashing out then dragging out innocent bystanders
Charged with public order offences under false pretences

Nicked by Old Bill grabbed by the fuzz
Brut Musk no need to discuss much
Save your protestations for Judge Grudge

Big Ron's a tosser gis a job Yosser
Thrown in the back of a black mariah van battered by rozzas
Given first aid back at the pig station
By more tolerant officers
Something is happening and it's happening right now

The final whistle has gone one last vitriolic song
Then the snarling throng of bad losers spew out from this
Dump of a ground onto grimly lit
Recession hit coronation streets
To be met by a thin blue line of sadistic bizzies
And wildly excited alsatian dogs straining at the leash

Petty criminals delinquent thugs
Hell bent on causing havoc and for opportunities to loot
Mounted officers re-enact Peterloo
As if they needed an excuse
All coppers are bastards until otherwise proved
Moody youths testosterone fuelled spoiling for a fight
Train station to the left buses to the right
Hooligan the scourge of postmodern times
A chance to agitate participate in a wider political dispute

Dino Zoff it's all kicked off we've broken through the cordon
Earl's a winger Pearl's a singer my favourite song
Is entitled boredom
Now I find myself caught up in the cauldron
Of violent disorder
Grimacing faces contorted with hatred
Bulldog tattoos Doc Marten boots symbolic red laces
Dark satanic mills God forsaken places
Going toe to toe bouncing on pavements
Windmilling hit in hope handbags at ten paces

Some scallywag lad put our coach window through with a
Brick then fled from the attack
A three star jumper half way up his back
Like shit off a stick away he ran faster than
Greased lightning man
All the way back home the freezing wind raged
Throughout the compartment put an end to all the craic
I would give everything I own for a warm Crombie coat
Instead of this piss wet through designer anorak

Going Underground selling England by the pound
Looking for trouble 50 head-hunters came to town
Keith Brown alone stood his ground glory shone around
That drew a round of applause
From the slavering Chelsea hordes
Entered into folklore where splodgenessabounds

Some look in dustbins for something to eat
They find a dead rat think it's a treat
Some hang monkeys others drug dependent thieves
Often inclined to sexually engage with unlucky sheep
The rest of youse are cocky twats I am dirty Leeds
Identity is the crisis can't you see? My girl's mad at me

Bradford Hillsborough led the way to present day nanny state
For the greater good the beautiful game was saved
Now it's big business and players' agents who call the shots
And through the nose all must pay
For prawn sandwiches replica shirts tired clichés
It's a game of 2 halves at the end of the day

What ever happened to The Stranglers?
When I hear certain songs I look back in Wranglers
And reminisce from afar with misty eyed nostalgia
Remembering the thrill when the world stood still
At 3 o'clock each Saturn's day
From the end of August right through to early May

Away days playing chase the ace
With Mad Cyril and Voodoo Ray
$E = MC2$ anger is an energy
Even after all these years scratch the surface
Undivided tribal loyalty remains
Not a way of life as such more a right of way
I blame the parents Gabba Gabba Hey

Anybody seen Ashy

School of hard knocks Guantanamo shocks
I'm looking for a Rastafarian in Whitelocks
He could be in Beeston or EEP
Working at the door of the Skyrack Headingley
Could be in Jamaica or Islamabad
Could be Hamas could be Mossad
In Chapeltown for a Tridentine mass
A brand new convertible is out of my class

He said something about a Yardie
Watching Laurel and Hardy
3 men to a cell in a prison called Armley
Pianorama a black and white drama
The thief the fool the gambler
In Pax Americana

Second Generation just like me
Doing the Haka with Stewart outside Jacomellis
Divine nation Royal Park after dark
Watching Michelangelo's vital spark
Inflationary universe Burley Road
Feels like the streets are gonna implode
Kobayashi king of the Jews
I'm searching for a minotaur and his muse.

Playing them songs all night long
Boom diddy boom diddy
Boom boom boom diddy

He lost a brother in the Istanbul night
He lost another who took his own life
Men killing God God killing men
Modus operandi no comprende my friend

Ancient mariner washed up on the rocks
How come one shepherd own all the flocks
Hey good looking what you got cooking
You're going home in an ambulance

Mother Shipton Abel and Cane
The second coming on Harehills Lane
Stardust memories shared history
Assimilation in the land of the free
So take it to the door Halton Moor
The Prophet has left LS14
Belle Isle believes string of beads
Sowing them seeds in the fields of Athenry

Anybody seen Ashy
Burley Road Ashy?

Ode to Joy

Cometh the hour
For the ashes of your Fathers
And the temples of your Gods
Ode to Joy

A Celtic tiger playing for England
Everywhere is conflict everything is a contradiction
Heard the sound of distant drums mothers give up your sons
Old men have declared war and youth must fight and die

I am the dreamer who lived the dream
A one man army battalion of me
Fighting for survival await my arrival
At the height of the fighting I salute you my rival

Crocodile tears
The loudest patriots
Are the greatest profiteers

Hail Caesar let slip the dogs of war
Transform this dirt poor troubadour into a tour de force
Defender of empire state master of my fate
Captain oh my Captain our enemy is at the gate

Promises that I must keep
Miles to go before I sleep
Paladin on the Somme Armageddon
Trailing clouds of glory still they come

A thousand yard stare
Trembling there
On the brink of insanity

In my arena conflict is theatre
Across the Steppe we drive nobody here gets out alive
A face that launched a thousand ships truth sits upon thy lips
Stare in to the abyss ignorance is bliss

Hit the ground running destruction so stunning
Whom the Gods love die young
Always be ready steady boys steady
We fight we conquer again and again

Love and devotion
Washing our boots in the Indian Ocean

Widow maker media writer
One mans terrorist is another mans freedom fighter
A starving man at his master's gate
Predict the ruin of the state
Man is born free but everywhere he is in chains

There can be no peace 'til everyman is free
There is no sin but stupidity
There is a church there is a steeple
Six feet of earth make all men equal

At the stetting of the sun the Valkyrie have sung
Götterdämmerung

Boy soldier marching through Georgia
Love and devotion boys will be boys
From Atlanta to the sea

To save your world you asked this man to die
Would this man could he see you now ask why?

There aint nothing more peaceful than a dead man

Death Warmed Up

Flippin' heck
Who took the bolts out of your neck
Are you a relative of Shrek
Or some woebegone Klingon with no bling on
Slung out of Star Trek?

Hideous grotesque unwashed unblessed
Death obsessed a man possessed
An inbred with a misshapen head
I look into the bathroom mirror see myself
Staring back at the living dead

In catacombs I lick my wounds
Ponder the subtle differences between
The mean reds and the blues
Discarded grots sweaty socks contribute
To the all-pervading reek of miasmic perfume

Bruised confused not fit for purpose no longer of use
Self reflect on my own unique set of interpersonal issues
Ugly episodes no win scenarios
Scrunching man sized snotty tissues
Chronic self neglect little self respect
My nearest and dearest have all upped and left

I have taken to my bed much prefer to hide away instead
Reading extracts from Ecclesiastes to soothe
The savage breast
In distress I reside in a midden of my own detritus
Laid prostrate my own fate I try second guess
Only wanted to be loved not face this acid test
Terror management theory is what I do best

Wired depressed no right to happiness
Sick and tired of being sick and tired
Everything is meaningless
Riddled with doubt tortured by regret
I am the baddest man in dismal land I buried all the rest

The grim reaper and the four horsemen
Wait in the other room
I heard them speak in no uncertain terms
That I am to be discontinued
They say embrace death each must perish all must die
Me that doth include
Come this time tomorrow I'll be yesterday's fake news
Fuck 'em all feed 'em rice is my couldn't care less attitude

Canterbury Trails

In the summer of 2015 out of the blue
An opportunity appeared to further careers
Keep the wolves from the door pay off tax arrears
Failure is not an option if we are to restore the golden years

Harnessing all the energy and collective experience we could
Muster no time for small talk plenty for bluster
Working nights away from home has lost some of its gloss
But the lure of filthy lucre lost none of its lustre
We are going darn sarf to the garden of England
On an 8 week project
Hoping for general success not General Custer

To keep ourselves in jobs we formed angry mobs
So me, Simon Martin and Charlie Rhodes
Went forward into battle with drill bit Taylor
Our Napoleonic boss
Together we are a brotherhood of likeable rogues
A company of electrical engineers getting paid to give a toss

Chose to enlist persist co-exist
In rented accommodation where love it don't live
3 dimensional curves in a world of twist
Shouting out quotes from The Exorcist
The power of the risen one defies the laws of physics

Each have a room eat convenience food
All share a house with bad feng shui
But it is the only one available in the immediate vicinity
So we'll just have to make do
Unfinished sympathy I have taken up the recovery position
On the other side of the gloom

Incognito in too deep all my blankets in a heap
A suburban robot that monitors reality
Pretending I'm not me
A self-loathing self-pitying little creep
Sat here alone charging my phone wondering what kind of
Clientele frequent the Club Chemistry

Who will rid me of this turbulent priest
That made a desert called it peace
When the coin in the coffer rings the soul from limbo springs
The pardoners take money to stave off the beast
The peasants are revolting in death they are released
I have travelled from ye olde Leodis to haunt these medieval
Streets a daemon to appease

Severe mental test unidentified flying Chaucer's overhead
Which came first the chicken or the egg
I'm not the sharpest tool in the shed
12 hour shifts a microwave meal then straight back to bed
Beating myself up for being easily led

Component parts broken hearts conduit and tray
Wage slaves from rival trades must negotiate a way
Put aside our differences try cooperate
To ensure completion by the given date
Because the fear of class action punitive sanctions
Are too severe to contemplate

Schrodinger's cat brain in a vat what's it like to be a bat?
There's a fire alarm fault somewhere in this gaff
It's 4 in the morning yawning has broken
Too much pressure understaffed
Northern monkeys here to suffer no doubt about that
No refuge in the Kessel from the massive attack

Traffic wardens prowling the streets
Strictly enforcing edicts of the powers that be
The pilgrims fall silent read them and weep
The natives are restless the seagulls don't sleep
The homeless huddle in shop doorways trying to compete
With wandering minstrels wannabe Joe Strummers
And vagabond drummers that seldom skip a beat

Operation Stack
The M20 has ground to a halt
Swarms of economic migrants refuse to turn back
But I don't worry myself with pulp fiction
When presented as fact
I keep myself busy coping with dizzy my head is spinning
Trying to keep my faculties together
And multiple personalities intact

The thought of hiding in a refrigerated articulated vehicle for
Long duration in complete darkness
With five inches of face space slowly freezing to death
Fills me with dread
Makes me break out in ice cold claustrophobic sweat
Inducing nightmarish visions I would much rather forget

Empty motorways long night time drives
Dartford Tunnel state of mind
Appreciating this great nation's engineering feats
Infrastructure street furniture skilful enterprise
Grateful to Angela Elaine for logistical support digs organised
And valuable contributions given by Ross Bainbridge at
Critical times

A big shout out to Mark at CEF
Reference Natwest always gave of his best
Toothy grin stubbly chin where's flip flop? he'd ask in jest
In snatched conversations we discovered a mutual likeness
For dance music DJ EZ did the rest

Where are you boys heading next?
Sittingbourne or Maidstone teaming up with Super Mario,
Daz Westerman and evil genius Matty O
But we haven't had official confirmation yet cho
He said take care boys seez yer laters bros
Each in turn we shook his hand wished him all the best
Then the 3 amigos took the exit left

When you're in a pickle call John McNicholl
It's party time and any old hubris will do
We have gathered in the Carpenters Arms hidden from view
Sat drinking beer stood playing pool
Toasting the success of the rock steady crew
Finished on time we saw the job through
It's a fine line between triumph and defeat
Medway between the two

In the grounds of the Cathedral I sat awhile each day
Said a prayer for you
Because to whisper holy words under my breath
Is all that I can do
Together we witnessed the collapse of the old order
And the shock of the new
My dear Ave Maria work saveth this man
But it sure is a big scary world without you

The Ontological Argument

My God can beat the devil out of your God
Throws thunderbolts with ease
He alone is spiritual perfection
Did not evolve from chimpanzees

He eats Mars for breakfast Galaxies for tea
Is merciful to sinners ignores the pleas of amputees
He warms the bed on a frosty night
And suffocates all the fleas

Recently whilst attempting to negotiate my way
Through the morality maze of present day
In heightened states did stop awhile to contemplate
That if God's message is salvation why speak of separation
Retaliation eternal damnation in theatres of hate
Only a dictator would point a finger of blame
Require unspeakable acts be done in thy name
A warrior king divide and rule
Distort the truth the light the way

Project fear a pub with no beer
Doubts have appeared cracks in the veneer
Fracturing the cultural bedrock of all I hold dear
Why will me into existence then from the moment of
Conception try make me disappear
My smart phone has developed feelings
The stars don't know I'm here

I struggle with the idea that an omnipotent creator
Here there everywhere the grand designer of la misère
Could sit in judgement verdict declare
Grant me redemption or eternal despair
Pretending to have no prior inclination to the culmination of
Events if all the whilst was there
Why would any master of the universe give a damn or even
Care if all along knew the outcome of the entire sordid affair?

I question the authority of self-appointed self-anointed
Messianic types to speak of Übermensch preach draconian
Codes for life from spiteful holy books filled with kryptonite
Swallowed up whole by Zombie like acolytes fed the lie
That in the grand scheme of holographic simulation by
Artificial means they alone hold the bragging rights
To an exclusive version of a utopian dream
Amidst the confusion I have arrived at the conclusion
Religion is socialism farting however blasphemous to some
That may seem

Schism mind blowing decisions head on collisions
Highway to hell road to perdition
Which coping mechanism which ethical prison
Is the more righteous path
Abraham or Brahman fairy tales of the ancients taken as fact
A patriarchal figure sat on a cloud
Who looks like yer dad?

Which invisible friend no beginning no end
Which opiate to best sedate the masses
Stifle meaningful debate
Where is the evidence incontrovertible proof
Show me this demiurge that hides in clear view
Should I fear the reaper or look a little deeper
For patterns in the emergent pixilated truth?

Wishful thinking leap of faith for the sake of future days
No sympathy no affinity with any kind of brain washed
Zionist unscientific Scientologist non-specific narcissist
Or life of Brian fantasist
No pity for the Jihadist that sacrificed everything
Paid the ultimate price to rid the world of jinn
Who now resides in Jahannam with 79 nagging virgins
Not one will copulate with him

Secular moral philosophy in a fair and caring
Wealth sharing society is how it should and ought to be
I am comforted by the thought that I am living a life
No saviour worth his salt would condemn
Could not forgive or disagree

On the balance of all known possibilities
I choose to believe in me
Be the best version of myself I can possibly be
Encourage my latently suppressed altruistic tendencies
Arrest temptation toward normalisation of unchecked desire
For the sole purpose of self-aggrandisement
When faced with the darkly stark options
Between personal hell or blood libel
I go with earthly purgatory

Never ending story the filth the fury
Gravitational forces pulled apart by crazy horses
Mine eyes have seen the glory
No greater sinner than me

A colony of fire ants float merrily down the stream
Selfless concern for the welfare of others life is but a dream
Dance joyous cosmology a message to you Rumi
Life's grim contest is all everything changes but trees

So if there's no afterlife no pearly gates
Or day of reckoning be
Ain't no big deal no great shakes
All is well that ends with me

Postscript

Too legit to quit at the risk of chattin' shit
May I humbly posit an altar native ontological priori
A layman's attempt to reason rationalise
The staggering complexities of cause and effect
The subjective perspective of an autodidact
Concerning the nature of being and the ghost in the tesseract

A response to age old questions who made me what went
Bang where do I fit in with the scheme of the plan?
The frank opinions of testosterone fuelled nostro uomo
Vitruvian Man
The whole caboodle enchilada shouting match shebang
It took 13.7 billion years for me to get here
I feel therefore I am

Walking tall stood erect
Displaying nefarious characteristics of the one hundredth
Monkey effect
A critique ascertained through patient inquiry
Deduced from common sense full blown
Stockholm syndrome sentient homo sapien life experience
Love of wisdom out there on the road
Eeking out a meagre living in this unforgiving Holocene
Epoch of great uncertainty for reasons yet unknown

Cold hard facts opposites attract no more terrible secrets
Challenging conventional wisdom traditional narratives
Conspiracy theories urban myths
A work of staggering genius
A mad rant stating the bleedin' obvious
Not too easily dismissed
A pointless exercise away with the faeries
That's just the way it is

Holy gnosis smell the neurosis
A general theory of everything
From osmosis to Chris Moses
A whiff of fresh air to neutralise dragon breath nullify
Dogmatic halitosis
Which offend the chemoreceptor sensory cells that live up
People's noses

Treatise origin of species
An uncorrupted thesis redolent of love
A reconfiguration of all the pieces in the puzzle
Oh Lord please don't let me be misunderstood
Bridge the divide between lost tribes and gentiles
Reunite Sunnis Shiites loony left brigade alt right troglodytes
Lonely pantheists eighth stage atheists satanists creationists
Infidels Jedi knights
Reinvigorate the lives of all ye agnostic tykes with immaterial
Gripes that cherry pick the best bits
From star sign premium lines

Welcome back to the light you I have missed
Everybody welcome you're all on the list
It's the best disco in town called live and let live
Come on everybody let's do the twist

Sisters brothers to each other be kind
Bow heads together in praise of penicillin
The miracle of modern times
Be mindful that the chance of viable apocalyptic antibiotic
Mutation misuse is high
The geek shall inherit the earth if the rest of youse don't mind
Take responsibility seize control of the primeval fury raging
In your own savage soul
If we aint trading we are at war
All we are we leave behind

Calling all earthlings weak and strong
Ye Whites ye Wongs tumultuous throng
So very precious capable of such beauty each and every one
Imitate good do unto others as you would have done
Let revenge be the laughter of your children
There is no thing higher than you
Limitless undying love shines before us like a million suns
Whispers continue after we are gone
Peace unity justice apes together strong

Exponential mind expansion DNA coded strands
Fetch in more wood fetch in more sand
Create better versions of ourselves
Evolution is pitiless all merciful is man

We are dead stars looking back at the sky
Intuitive manipulative highly developed thrill seeking
Organisms wanting to ride the lightning
Scheming for a brighter future better things to come
Terraforming transforming into a supreme being ad infinitum
In the relative proportions of 9:3:3:1
Tetragrammaton thy will be done
Type three civilisation the race has begun

Simply put it is this
God is a work in progress
Alpha omega now is it
Doppler shift big picture incomplete
It aint over till its over
If you catch my red drift

Until such time as trans humankind can overcome death
Transcend cosmic consciousness go beyond miraculous
Become biocentric infinity machines that can access dreams
Waves particles everywhere at once
Traverse the multiverse quantum loop
In cahoots with the absolute
Decode the finer details in the Akashic gobbledygook
Know the total sum of all that was is yet to be
And in this moment is
One in blissful union with the entire anamnesis of each
And every carbon and silicon based entity that ever lived
Then shall divine exist

Enlightenment is the complete eradication
Of everything we imagine to be true
To understand the meaning is to live forever

God is knowledge in our hands
Serving creativity at peace with itself
Trying to get by with a little help from its friends
Make order from chaos a world without end
In memory of memory

Amen

38783777R00035

Printed in Poland
by Amazon Fulfillment
Poland Sp. z o.o., Wrocław